C000056081

Oliver Bertram's Barnato-Hassan special was first raced in 1934. It was fitted with an 8 litre Bentley engine running on a blend of alcohol, benzole and petrol. Originally only rear-wheel brakes were fitted but, as this picture of the car in action shows, the braking has been modernised. The intrepid driver is Keith Schellenberg.

MOTORING SPECIALS

Ian Dussek

Shire Publications Ltd

CONTENTS

ACKNOWLEDGEMENTS

Much assistance in the production of this Album was kindly provided by the National Motor Museum, Beaulieu. All the photographs are reproduced by permission of the National Motor Museum.

Printed in Great Britain by C. I. Thomas & Sons (Haverfordwest) Ltd, Press Buildings, Merlins Bridge, Haverfordwest, Dyfed SA61 1XF.

British Library Cataloguing in Publication Data: Dussek, Ian. Motoring specials. 1. Cars. Construction. I. Title. 629.23. ISBN 0-7478-0118-5.

Editorial Consultant: Michael E. Ware, Curator of the National Motor Museum, Beaulieu.

Cover: *A classic example of the special builder's art: John Bolster's twin motorcycle-engined car 'Bloody Mary', on display at the National Motor Museum, Beaulieu. Built by two schoolboys for driving round a field, 'Bloody Mary' developed into one of the most potent sprint and hillclimb cars ever built.*

Below: *The Vauxhall Villiers: Raymond Mays, Peter Berthon and Amhurst Villiers produced this powerful special in 1928 around a supercharged 1922 TT Vauxhall 3 litre engine. In Mays's hands it dominated speed hillclimbing in the early 1930s.*

A roadgoing special: the Nordec Special, fitted with a supercharged 1100 cc Ford engine. The supercharger is cunningly shrouded by the spotlamp cowl on the nearside of the bonnet and refashioning of the Ford Anglia radiator grille gives the Nordec the appearance of a BMW. Alongside at Silverstone in 1954 is a Mark VI Lotus, clearly showing the modifications Colin Chapman made to traditional Ford front suspension.

THE SPECIAL

This book describes some of the efforts of many individuals to build their own cars. A 'special' is essentially a one-off design, built for the satisfaction of its constructor. The reasons for doing so are many. Some of the more common are: to construct something different; to build a car which is not only competitive but which, owing to the constructor's ingenuity or technical talent, may be faster or otherwise able to beat the opposition; and to construct such a car within the designer's means, using components and materials which are to hand or easily obtainable.

The variations on these themes are infinite and no one factor is common to all. Count Zborowski spent thousands of pounds on his specials; John Bolster's cost £25. By and large, specials have been associated with impecunious designers.

Specials tend to be built for competitive driving; they tend to be transitory in that a special develops during its lifetime but in the event of an accident there is usually little to be lost by discarding it. Only recently have a few specials acquired an intrinsic value and even with these it may be financially advantageous to dismantle the special and 'restore' it to the original car from which the chassis, engine or other parts first came.

A special is not a prototype, that is a car which is designed with production in mind, although very occasionally a special is so good that it achieves commercial success. Similarly, because a production car is called a 'special' it may mean merely that it has sporty bodywork or improved performance.

By its very nature every special is unique, but over the years certain combinations of

3

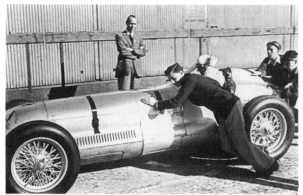

The Multi-Union: in 1938 Chris Staniland rebuilt his Tipo B eight cylinder 2.9 litre Alfa Romeo with improved independent suspension, supercharging and braking, and a body reminiscent of the Grand Prix Mercedes Benz. The car lapped Brooklands at over 140 mph (224 km/h), but development was halted by the Second World War, in which Staniland was killed. Today, significantly, the Alfa Romeo element of the car is considerably more valuable than the special.

components have been favoured by special builders.

The chassis, around which the special is built, tends to come from an old, discarded vehicle, especially a GN, an Austin Seven or one of various types of Ford, but anything from wooden beams to a Rolls-Royce has been used at one time or another. The chassis can be shortened (cut and shut), lengthened, slimmed, widened, drilled for lightness, strengthened or even turned upside down.

Suspension, that is the springing, shock absorbing and axles, is frequently taken from other vehicles or substantially modified. Previously solid front axles can be cut in half and relocated, and various methods of creating independent suspension have also been devised.

The engine and transmission offer unlimited opportunities, ranging from air-cooled motorcycle units to power units extracted from army tanks and bomber aircraft. The engine, sometimes driving through its original gearbox, by conventional propeller shaft, chain or even belt, may be extensively redesigned or totally replaced during the life of the special, to the considerable confusion of the motoring historian.

The body may range from total luxury to a cushion on the floorboards.

A special probably, but not always, has four wheels, a steering wheel and a power unit in a chassis or frame. Almost everything else is optional. The craft of special building flourished with the availability of conventional ladder chassis, commonly used in vehicle construction up to the 1960s, although the modern high-performance space frame stems substantially from special building. The construction of a special around a modern unitary shell is technically more complex and the older machines are those which tend to create the most interest. Further, modern regulations controlling the construction and use of vehicles do not encourage special builders.

The competitive events for which many of the specials were built fall into six major categories: circuit racing; sprints or speed trials; speed hillclimbs; trials; autocross; and auto or driving tests.

Circuit racing takes place at such venues as Brands Hatch and Silverstone, and specials are usually seen at the club meetings rather than the major events. These club events are run by one-make or local clubs and are a feature of the British sporting calendar. A racing special could be matched against similar vehicles conforming to a formula, for example based on engine size, a common power unit or on a handicap system based on estimated speed. In the last, the ingenuity of the special builder can be pitted against the handicapper more easily than in the case of a known make.

In sprints or speed trials the driver tries to cover a given distance in the shortest possible time, racing against the clock rather than other cars. One of the best known, which has fostered some very unusual specials, is that held on the Madeira Drive, Brighton, each year.

Speed hillclimbs work on the same prin-

4

The Halford Special: the aero-engine designer Frank Halford took an Aston Martin chassis as the basis of his racing car in 1925. The 1.5 litre motor had numerous refinements, including twin camshafts and, initially, an exhaust-powered turbocharger. Almost every car in this Brooklands picture is labelled 'special'.

For sprinting and hillclimbs, Frank Le Gallais acquired a 3.4 litre XK 120 engine from the Jaguar factory and built this rear-engined special. In 1952, as seen at Brighton, the car ran with twin carburettors and single rear wheels. By 1957 it featured a De Dion rear axle with twin rear wheels, plus an additional carburettor. Few specials remain for long in their original form.

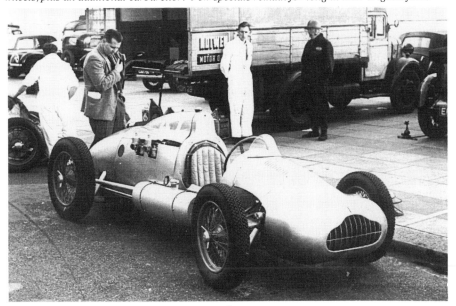

Above: *The Cornishman Ashley Cleave built this special out of a crashed 1938 Morris Eight saloon, installing a highly tuned and modified 1086 cc Morris Ten based engine. Despite its humble origins, the car was particularly successful in speed hillclimbs and is shown winning the 1100 cc class at Prescott in 1954, defeating two Coventry Climax powered Lotuses. Cleave won over five hundred awards, from trials to racing, and drove his Morris special to and from the events.*

Below left: *A trials special in action in 1954, showing the conditions of sporting trials. Steep gradients, tight corners and mud or rocks have to be tackled without stopping. This is the Ford 1172 cc based M and L Special, the product of Stirling Moss's father, Alfred, and trials exponent Mike Lawson. The M and L Special is now on display at the National Motor Museum.*

Below right: *Autocross provides comparatively low-cost competition for special builders. In recent years autocross has become less agricultural, but this picture of N. H. Overton in his Ford-based Overton Mark V at Farley Hill Autocross clearly illustrates the stresses of off-road speed events. This special was built with trials in mind.*

The heyday of the special: the paddock at Shelsley Walsh in the 1930s. A youthful John Bolster, hands on hips, can be seen behind car number 11, while number 10, with its air-cooled twin engine in a GN chassis, clearly shows the influence of Davenport.

ciple, but the course is constructed up a hill or drive, frequently with tortuous bends and short straights, calling for high performance from both car and driver. Since before the First World War the supreme test for special builders has been Shelsley Walsh hill, a 1000 yard (923 metre) course near Worcester.

In trials the car and driver are set to climb unsurfaced tracks or sections marked out on grassy slopes. These events come in various guises, such as for road-going cars, the best known of these being the Motor Cycling Club's Exeter, Land's End and Edinburgh trials. There is additionally a National Trials Car Formula governing cars eligible for the Royal Automobile Club Motor Sport Association British Sporting Car Trials Championship. Sporting trials are designed with specials in mind and the formula sets out the parameters within which such cars can be constructed, such as minimum wheelbase and maximum engine capacity.

Autocross is a version of the sprint, held on grass. Such events call for considerable low-speed torque and improved grip on rough and slippery surfaces.

Auto or driving tests require the driver to negotiate a series of obstacles, such as pylons and garages, in the fastest possible time without hitting the markers.

Other specials have been used in rallying and even *concours* shows.

It will be apparent that not only are the permutations endless but that many thousands of specials have been constructed over a century of motoring. This Album features some sixty representative or notable competition specials which have brought fame to their constructors. For practical purposes, these have been mainly limited to pre-1960 cars, having been built around or from the traditional components of chassis, engine and transmission.

7

A sports GN in production trim, driven by T. Gilmore Ellis at Sutton Bank hillclimb in 1920. The brakeless front axle is attached to the chassis by slender quarter elliptic springs and the cover for the chain drive is visible at the rear. The long bonnet houses an air-cooled V-twin; the 'radiator' is a dummy. The enormous mud flap under the front wing is a reflection of the state of road surfaces in the 1920s.

POPULAR SPECIALS

Specials have been built out of components from almost every car ever produced but some sources have proved particularly popular.

GN, FRAZER NASH AND HRG

In the early days of motoring the car was an expensive luxury for the very wealthy. Young and impecunious enthusiasts made do with motorcycles. By 1910 the concept of a quadricycle or cyclecar, in effect a four-wheel motorcycle, had become established, led by Archie Frazer-Nash and Ron Godfrey. On the strength of a single car built in a few days, they announced a range of production machines and the cyclecar movement was in being. Their GN cars were not, as such, specials but were to become the basis for some of the best known examples.

The GN chassis was based on two parallel straight channel sections with tubular front axle located by quarter elliptic springs and radius arms. The rear axle was solid, driven by a set of chains and sprockets of different ratios in place of the differential and gearbox. Brakes were fitted to the rear wheels. The rear axle was located on quarter elliptic springs. Power was provided by a V-twin air-cooled engine, initially parallel to the chassis rails, subsequently at 90 degrees to them. The first GNs were very basic, with sketchy bodies, but became more sophisticated and, of their kind, were reliable. They were also light and, because of their suspension, exceptional in performance and roadholding.

The GN flourished up to 1923 and several thousand were built, both in England and, under licence by Salmson, in France. However, with the coming of the Austin Seven and 'proper' small cars, they were discarded and became an invaluable source of components for special builders at minute cost — less than £10 for a complete car. It was

8

not the end of the GN heritage since Frazer-Nash started building cars in his own name and later Godfrey produced the HRG; both of these makes clearly showed their GN parentage.

Of the early GN specials, by far the greatest was *Spider*, designed and built by Basil Davenport. *Spider* started in 1923 as a conventional GN chassis, modified with central steering, plus a V-twin 1087 cc engine. A tall narrow single-seater body was fitted. In 1924 installation of a 1.5 litre engine made the car dramatically fast, for sprints, sand racing and hillclimbs. By 1927 *Spider* had taken the outright record for Shelsley Walsh and set fastest time of day there no fewer than seven times. The car was retired in the early 1930s but was preserved and brought out of retirement after the Second World War. Later Davenport constructed a replica, *Spider II*, using a specially designed HRG chassis from Ron Godfrey, fitted with a 2 litre engine.

Another early exponent was R. G. J. Nash, whose *Terror* and *Spook* specials were a combination of GN and Frazer Nash, with Anzani 1.5 litre engines. E. J. Moor's *Wasp* and E. G. Sharp's *Gnat* GNs were other variants on the theme.

The GN chassis, easily cut to the desired length, accommodated many different power units and transmissions. The front suspension was also frequently modified, either by substitution of the Morgan sliding pillar system or by linking the quarter elliptic springs to hydraulic or telescopic suspension units.

Specials were also built up on Frazer Nash chassis, of which the 2 litre AC-engined Semmence was one of the prettiest,

Right and below: *'Spider', Basil Davenport's amazing GN special, at the start of a special parade (right) at the Vintage Sports Car Club meeting at Oulton Park in 1961. Little has changed, apart from the minimal addition of headgear, in 34 years, as the 1927 picture (below) of 'Spider' setting a new course record at Shelsley Walsh in pouring rain shows.*

A FAMOUS CHAIN-DRIVEN SPORTS CAR— THE FRAZER-NASH

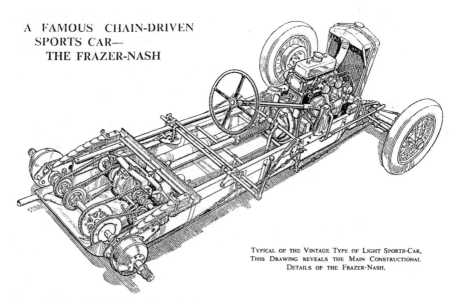

TYPICAL OF THE VINTAGE TYPE OF LIGHT SPORTS-CAR, THIS DRAWING REVEALS THE MAIN CONSTRUCTIONAL DETAILS OF THE FRAZER-NASH.

The principle of the GN chassis as developed in the Frazer Nash can clearly be seen, including the parallel channel frame and the chain-driven final drive alternative to the conventional gearbox. There is also differential transmission. Suspension at both front and rear is by quarter elliptic leaf springs.

'The Terror', R. G. J. Nash's first special, was an Anzani-engined Frazer Nash, whose power was developed to nearly 100 brake horsepower. It was modified at various times: for example, the radiator cowling was changed after the date of this picture, taken at Shelsley Walsh in 1931.

10

The Semmence special is a combination of Frazer Nash and a six-cylinder 2 litre AC engine. Cable brakes are retained and the lines of the car present an interesting comparison with those of the production Frazer Nash.

while in modern times Ron Footit's AC-GN has proved itself a highly competitive car in vintage racing.

The most interesting HRG special was the very short-lived Halford Cross Rotary, an offset single-seater powered by a highly sophisticated 1.5 litre rotary valve engine designed by R. C. Cross. Rotary valves are extremely difficult to seal and the car, although potentially very rapid, was unreliable, so its constructor, Ted Halford, dismantled it. Unlike most specials, the major components were not scrapped but recycled into a production HRG.

The combination of the six cylinder 2 litre AC engine and the GN chassis is extremely potent, as demonstrated by Ron Footit. The superstructure over the front axle supports the improved shock absorbers, requiring the steering arm and drag link to be re-routed under the front axle.

The Austin Seven formed the basis of thousands of specials. This 1925 version has minute four-wheel brakes, an early improvement on the original two-wheel system. Much of the 10 horsepower developed by the 747 cc engine must have been used compensating for the aerodynamics of the windscreen. Later models of the Austin Seven had a larger body frontal area and a lower windscreen.

AUSTIN SEVEN

Probably more specials have been constructed on the basis of the Austin Seven than all other specials put together. Sir Herbert Austin, on whose billiard table the car was designed, introduced the model (originally of 696 cc capacity) in 1922 and it remained in production for some fifteen years. During this time around 400,000 were built and developed from spindly pram-like vehicles to saloon cars in miniature. The Austin Seven was never particularly cheap; it was originally priced at £225, reducing steadily. By 1930 it cost £125. Production commenced in 1923 and it featured a chassis shaped like an A in plan, a three-speed gearbox and a simple rear axle. It was propelled by a 747 cc side-valve engine developing 10 brake horsepower. A self-starter was added later. The brakes tended to be nominal but were improved. The original cars were very light, weighing 800 pounds (364 kg) and were open. In time the power went up to 17 brake horsepower, but by that time heavier saloon bodies were fitted.

The Austin Seven appeared in many guises, some sporting, and even as a high-performance racing car. However, from the 1930s onwards, redundant Austin Sevens were readily available from scrapyards and became the basis for thousands of specials. This movement was fostered by the Seven Fifty Motor Club, formed in the late 1930s, which was responsible for organising competitions and encouraging amateur special builders in every possible way. It still does.

The Austin Seven engine was modified to produce increased power. An early development was the Gordon England overhead valve conversion. Although this produced more horsepower, the horn appears to be the most powerful-looking item.

The most primitive method of creating an Austin Seven special was to remove the body and build a new one, usually of a sporting nature, using materials ranging from building board to pre-stressed alloy panels. A second stage was to improve the suspension and brake performance by re-placing the primitive braking mechanism by fitting 'Bowdenex' cables or hydraulics.

Austin finally fitted effective brakes on the 1937 model. Attention to the engine could easily increase the power and, with im-proved roadholding and stopping power, the owner now had a sporting motor car. Many Austin Seven special builders went no further than this, but more serious engin-eers appreciated that these little cars had the potential for cheap and rapid motor sport.

A typical traditional Austin Seven special, built on a 1925 chassis, at Silverstone in 1954. The radiator is original but the wheels have been modified, the steering rake has been lowered and the slim body has necessitated the rearrangement of the handbrake externally.

13

One of the finest 750 specials ever built, the Lightweight Special, constructed in 1939 by Alec Issigonis and originally based on a supercharged Austin engine. The Lightweight Special featured rubber suspension, an aluminium-plywood sandwich body-chassis structure and extensive use of lightweight alloys.

During the 1950s and 1960s a number of manufacturers produced both mechanical and coachbuilders' accessories for Austin Seven enthusiasts. The wheels are smaller, but this fibreglass Ashley body, complete with hardtop, conceals the traditional Austin Seven chassis and power train.

14

This extraordinary Austin Seven based Haywood LHW special took the science of crab-tracking the wheels to extremes. In 1938 C. B. Lloyd designed this car for use in the International Six Day Motor Cycle Trial, exploiting a rule that two driven wheels could count as one, providing they were less than 1 foot (30 cm) apart. The Austin Seven rear axle was cut down to virtually the differential only.

By cutting the chassis length and reinforcing it with a tubular frame, the stability of the unit could be vastly improved.

Austin had drawn inspiration from the success of their engine to produce their own racing car; in its most advanced form it featured a twin overhead-camshaft layout with two-stage supercharging and developing 116 brake horsepower at 7600 revolutions per minute (rpm). However, amateurs realised that simple improvements in carburetion, special pistons and manifolding could all prove beneficial. Naturally there were problems with the increased power being transmitted via insufficiently strong two- and three-bearing crankshafts and slender connecting rods. Other items — radiators, water pipework, fuel feed and electrical components — all had to be modified if the special was to be a different shape from the original.

The interest in Austin Seven specials over the years has been such that many new and improved parts have been manufactured on a production basis, notably engines and running gear. Complete body kits, such as those manufactured by Cambridge Engineering Company, proved popular and during the 1950s glass-fibre body shells produced by Ashley and others were available. By the 1950s the inherent unsuitability of the chassis, compared with the power which could be extracted from improved versions of the engine, was such that it tended to be discarded in favour of space frames.

The Seven Fifty Motor Club provides comprehensive opportunities for racing specials based on the Austin Seven and its successor, the Reliant. Here is a field of assorted designs in action at Brands Hatch in 1961.

Left: *The extremely professional approach adopted by Charles Godsal is clearly visible in this illustration of his 1935 special, showing the unique chassis plate at the rear of the engine bay. The motor is Ford V8, albeit not the original.*

Below: *The chassis of Derek Buckler's 1947 Buckler Special under construction at Bucklers of Reading, showing the multi-tube space-frame chassis and the radiator mounted behind the Ford Ten engine. This prototype chassis design subsequently emerged as the basis of the Buckler Mark V Airflow model.*

A Batten Special with cabriolet bodywork, constructed for Lord Plunket in 1936. Batten Specials were useful trials performers and this one has considerable weight behind the rear axle, providing traction, possibly at the expense of roadholding.

FORD

During the 1930s designs based on the Ford V8 engine were popular. The V8 was introduced in 1932 and a number of constructors exploited its power by the simple process of lightening the chassis and substituting lightweight bodies. This combination was especially effective in trials. Some, such as Sydney Allard, got the balance right; on the other hand, the Batten Specials, based on the same formula, were difficult to handle at speed because of the flexibility of the chassis. A notable one-off, which might have entered production but for its cost, was the Godsal of 1935, a highly refined two-seater. The chassis was to Charles Godsal's own design, incorporating sliding pillar front suspension. The engine was a Ford V8, driving via a preselector gearbox to a Bentley rear axle, located by a Citroen transverse torsion bar. The car was bodied by Corsica, a leading sporting coachbuilder of the time, and might well have been considered a prototype if any other had followed or if Godsal had seriously contem-

plated manufacture. As the car cost some £3000 to construct, an enormous sum in 1935, its chances of success would have been minimal.

In 1935 Ford of Britain introduced an upgraded version of the £100 Y Type 'Eight', this having a 10 horsepower engine based on an 1172 cc four-cylinder unit with a bore of 63.5 mm and a stroke of 92.5 mm, developing 30 brake horsepower. This remained in use for 27 years in a variety of models, including the Ten, Anglia, Prefect, Popular and Escort. It was capable of a little over 60 mph (90 km/h) in standard trim. Like the Austin Seven, the 1172 cc Ford was available cheaply in very large numbers, as in production the cars had a much shorter life than their mechanical components. The modest performance of the engine could be raised in a series of simple steps. Its beauty lay in that it would rev easily up to 5500 rpm and had a low brake horsepower for its piston area. An increase of 30 per cent in power and an extra 1000 rpm could be obtained by using double valve springs and twin carburettors and raising the compression ratio. This could be increased dramatically, proportionate to the reduction in the weight of the car. The engine could also be supercharged.

Prominent amongst Ford Ten competition pioneers was Derek Buckler, who developed tubular chassis design. Buckler marketed multi-tube frames, independent suspension conversion units and a variety of accessories, including close ratio gears. Later complete cars in kit form were produced, which were popular and successful in club racing. Another effective trials special based on the Ford Ten was the *Dellow*, conceived by Ken Delingpole and Ron Lowe. This also went into limited production.

By the early 1950s the Ford-based specials dominated trialling, being extremely nimble and compact. One of the most unusual Ford specials, however, did not use a Ford engine at all. In 1950 Leslie Onslow-Bartlett used a Ford V8 transmission shaft as the basis of his chassis. The front axle was inverted Ford Ten, the gearbox Ford Eight and the differential Ford V8, other portions of the drive including Ford half shafts and chains. The rear-mounted engine was a fully race-prepared 996 cc JAP air-cooled unit, extracted from a Cooper — all this in a trials special. It was not as wonderful as its designer intended, a major problem being that with all the weight over and behind the rear axle there was little to keep the front down to steer the car.

The 1172 cc Ford was used as the basis of many specials during the 1950s and 1960s, and just as the Austin Seven formed the basis of the Seven Fifty formula so the Ford Ten was the basis of the 1172 series.

The Dellow was a Ford Ten based competition special which was popular enough to go into limited production. Despite its qualities, A. G. Parsons has had to resort to outside assistance on this West Country trial in 1952.

18

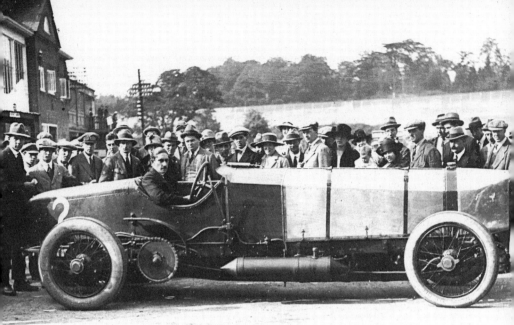

The first 'Chitty-Bang-Bang', with Count Louis Zborowski, at Brooklands, where its best lap speed was 113.45 mph (182.66 km/h).

VERY SPECIAL SPECIALS

CHITTY-BANG-BANG

The best known of all specials is *Chitty-Bang-Bang*, the car in the film *Chitty-Chitty-Bang-Bang* taking its name from three actual machines which were the brainchild of Count Louis Zborowski, a keen and wealthy racing motorist in the early 1920s. His design of specials was particularly significant in that it pioneered the concept of fitting an aero-engine into an automobile chassis. Zborowski shoehorned a 23 litre Maybach engine, developing some 300 horsepower, as used in German bombers, into an old Mercedes chassis. Drive was via a Mercedes gearbox with chain final drive.

The first *Chitty* had such brute power that it needed nearly 800 pounds (363 kg) of sand over the rear wheels to hold it down — but it proved an instant success at Brooklands, lapping at over 100 mph (161 km/h) and with a maximum speed of around 120 mph (193 km/h). During 1921 Zborowski had many Brooklands successes with the car although it was also driven on the roads, especially after suitable shock absorbers had been fitted.

Later in the year a second *Chitty* was constructed, using an 18,882 cc Benz aero-engine, again in a pre-1914 Mercedes chassis. Unlike *Chitty I*, which was purely a racing car, *Chitty II* was fitted up as a four-seater touring car. It raced at Brooklands in the autumn but could not beat the handicappers, despite lapping at over 108 mph (176 km/h).

Zborowski meanwhile began a third *Chitty*, based on a then current 28/95 Mercedes which he had recently purchased. The 7.25 litre engine was removed and replaced with a 14.8 litre Mercedes engine from a German First World War fighter. *Chitty III*, unlike *I* and *II*, had conventional shaft drive. It was completed in 1923.

In the meantime Zborowski still used *Chitty I*. The *Chittys* were hard on their tyres and in September 1922 a front tyre burst at speed at Brooklands, removing the front axle. As a result the Count did not race again at Brooklands with that particular car. He built one more special, the Higham Special, which had a V12 Liberty engine and later achieved fame as *Babs*, the land speed-record contender in which J. G. Parry Thomas lost his life on the Pendine Sands. *Chitty II* and *Babs* survive.

BLOODY MARY

Zborowski, who was killed in the 1924 Italian Grand Prix, was a rich man. John Bolster and his brother Richard were not wealthy but in 1929 as schoolboys they took a 760 cc JAP V-twin motorcycle engine, put it in a wooden chassis and connected it via a chain to a gearbox and thence to the rear wheels by a rubber belt. This rudimentary single-seater ran bodyless and cost some £25 to build. It did not steer well and wheels fell off, but gradually improvements were made: the front suspension became substantially GN, a better JAP engine was obtained, and the car was sufficiently legal to be driven to events such as hillclimbs. Component after component was improved, all in the original wooden chassis, by now well reinforced. An even more powerful 981 cc JAP engine followed, made available as a result of a motorcycle accident.

By 1933 Bolster had improved the transmission. The car was now highly competitive for speed hills, through careful engine tuning and equally careful choice of gearing to suit each particular course. Other less conventional methods of increasing power included emptying the sump immediately before starting a trial run, there being sufficient oil to lubricate the engine for a minute of motoring.

For 1934, again as a result of a motorcycle accident, Bolster acquired a second V-twin JAP engine. The two were linked, giving a four-cylinder 2 litre car weighing 784 pounds (356 kg), and by this time reasonably effective braking was installed. *Bloody Mary*, as the Bolster special was called, was highly competitive for the next two seasons. Bolster then designed an even more potent vehicle, a four-engined sprint machine. However, unlike many other specials,

The 23,092 cc six-cylinder engine of 'Chitty 1' was started by means of an aeroplane half-axle used as a lever. The starting magneto mounted in the cockpit had to be turned over at the same time by a second mechanic.

Zborowski and Clive Gallop constructed another aero-engined car, the Higham Special, using a 27 litre V12 Liberty unit. Renamed 'Babs', it was used by Parry Thomas for attempts on the world land speed record. In 1927 it crashed on the Pendine Sands, killing Parry Thomas, and was buried. However, in 1969 it was dug up and restored.

John Bolster expanded on the 'Bloody Mary' formula (as shown on the front cover) in 1938 by building a 4 litre four-engined special, using two JAP engines temporarily borrowed from 'Mary' and two more. The chassis incorporated independent front suspension. Here it is in action at Shelsley Walsh in 1938.

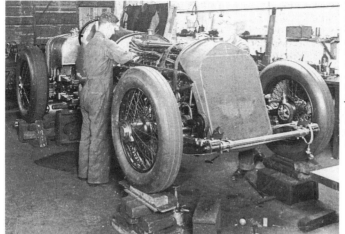

The Napier-Railton under construction at Thomson and Taylor's Brooklands premises in 1933. The huge Hartford friction shock absorbers are mounted in front of the front axle. A 65 gallon (295 litre) fuel tank is mounted above the double-cantilever rear springs.

Bloody Mary was not cannibalised and lay unwanted in a barn until 1945, when it was disinterred and started winning again. A racing accident in 1948 brought about Bolster's retirement from active competition and *Bloody Mary* is now preserved in the National Motor Museum at Beaulieu, generously loaned by his widow.

NAPIER RAILTON

The Napier Railton was designed for circuit racing at Brooklands by Reid Railton to the order of John Cobb in 1933. Cobb aimed to achieve lap speeds above 140 mph (225 km/h) on this notoriously bumpy circuit. The 10 foot 10 inch (3.25 metre) wheelbase chassis had a twelve-cylinder 24 litre Napier

Variations on a four-wheel theme: the 27 litre 'Swandean Spitfire' Special, built around a Rolls-Royce Merlin aero-engine, alongside the 250 cc motorcycle-engined Bennett Special at Brighton Speed Trials in 1956.

Lion aero-engine. Suspension was semi-elliptic at the front and double-cantilever at the rear. The Gurney Nutting bodywork was offset single-seat. Braking was rear-wheel only. From 1933 to 1939 Cobb's car dominated Brooklands racing and was also successful in record breaking between 1 kilometre and 24 hours. The Napier Railton set the all-time Brooklands lap record at 143.44 mph (230.84 km/h). It won the British Racing Drivers Club '500' race twice — 500 miles in 1935 and 500 kilometres in 1937. After the Second World War the car was used for film work and parachute testing, before being acquired by Patrick Lindsay, who restored it, fitting disc brakes to enable it to be used in modern circuit racing.

THE *SWANDEAN SPITFIRE* AND *FLYING TRIANGLE*

These two amazing specials were constructed around scrap aero-engines following the Second World War. The *Swandean Spitfire* was designed by Michael Wilcock, using a 27 litre Rolls-Royce Merlin 25 supercharged engine, originally intended for a Mosquito fighter bomber. This was installed in a chassis formed of two Daimler Scout car chassis welded together and was driven through a Daimler Double Six gearbox, reputedly from a royal limousine. Wilcock, who ran the Swandean garage at Worthing, West Sussex, used the car principally at the Brighton speed trials, achieving around 150 mph (240 km/h) at the end of the standing kilometre.

The *Swandean's* main rival, also aero-engined, was the *Flying Triangle* special, constructed by Ted Lloyd Jones and fitted with a Rolls-Royce Kestrel engine. The chassis was a single Daimler Scout car and the Kestrel merely 21 litres with four-wheel drive through a reversed Vauxhall gearbox. Although extremely difficult to drive, the *Flying Triangle* had considerable success, including fastest run at Brighton in 1952, but was scrapped to provide the engine for the restoration of a Hawker Hart biplane.

The 'Flying Triangle' Special's 21 litre engine, mounted behind the driver's seat, made the car extremely difficult to drive in speed hillclimbs, but Ted Lloyd Jones somehow controlled his creation, winning the over 3000 cc class and the award for fastest special at Shelsley Walsh in 1950. It is shown in action at Prescott in September 1952, the week after establishing fastest time of day at the Brighton Speed Trials.

'*Tiger Kitten*': *the Lones team preparing the car before a run. The Morgan-inspired front suspension is clearly visible, as is the 500 cc JAP power unit. Unlike many 'five hundreds' the engine was cowled in.*

MOTORCYCLES AND 'FIVE HUNDREDS'

The concept of using an air-cooled motorcycle engine to power a car is almost as old as motoring and the GN and many cyclecars used large V-twin engines. A notable small-engined pioneer was the 1925 *Jappic*, based on a 350 cc JAP and built by H. M. Walters. It weighed some 440 pounds (200 kg) all up and was capable of 70 mph (113 km/h). Beautifully streamlined, it took a number of world records in its class.

Later, in the 1930s, a highly sophisticated 1100 cc four-wheel chain-driven design, the *Skirrow*, was produced, using a very short chassis. Another notable machine was the 1936 *Freikaiserwagen*, built by David Fry and Dick Caesar, which was an amalgam of GN and Morgan with a V-twin Anzani engine set in Morgan style across the chassis. This was replaced with an 1100 cc Blackburn engine, which was subsequently supercharged. In 1947 the chassis

was changed and the following year an even lighter unit fitted, with the engine, now two-stage supercharged, turned 90 degrees in the chassis, driving through a Norton gearbox. In this guise the *Freikaiserwagen* took the record at Shelsley Walsh in 1950 but its driver was killed in an accident at Blandford later that year and the car was never used again.

Another pre-war motorcycle-engine exponent was Clive Lones with his *Tiger Cat* and *Tiger Kitten* specials, featuring a variety of JAP engines from 350 to 1000 cc, both in racing and hillclimbs. Whereas the *Freikaiserwagen* had its engine behind the driver, Lones put his at the front, in an Austin Seven van chassis turned upside down. An Austin Seven gearbox was also used. The car was developed considerably over the years but was best known in 500 cc form.

24

The forerunner of the movement: in 1925 H. M. Walters built the Jappic, powered by a 350 cc JAP engine, for both racing and record breaking. The ultra-slim 2¹/2 inch (62 mm) tyres reduced rolling resistance to a minimum.

During the Second World War enthusiasts in the West of England devised a 500 cc racing formula, later known as Formula III. The aim was to provide low-cost racing based on 500 cc motorcycle engines and transmission. A club was formed and by 1947 a number of cars had been built to a basic design consisting of a 500 cc unsupercharged motorcycle engine and minimum 500 pounds (227 kg) unladen weight.

Colin Strang's special can be described as the first successful 'five hundred' and established the conventional rear-engined layout plus motorcycle chain and gearbox transmission to a solid rear axle. Fiat Topolino transverse front suspension was used with power from a Vincent-HRD engine, running on alcohol. Strang tackled the problem of having a fixed engine driving an axle which moved, causing the chain to twist, eventually resolving it with torsion

The extraordinary 'Skirrow' special featured four-wheel drive, powered by a twin-cylinder motorcycle engine and transmitted via a complex arrangement of chains and clutches. It was designed for racing on loose dirt tracks, such as those used by speedway motorcycles.

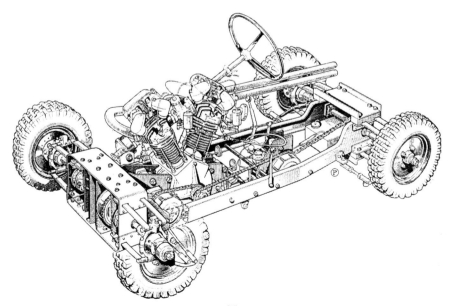

25

The 'Freikaiser-wagen' was first constructed in 1936 and was the subject of continual development. In its immediate post-war format, it still featured a GN based chassis, with the V-twin super-charged Blackburn engine mounted across the frame. Subsequently the GN chassis was replaced by a tubular design, the weight being reduced to 370 pounds (168 kg).

rods. Hydraulic brakes were also fitted. Virtually all subsequent 'five hundreds' followed the Strang pattern, even to the 'megaphone' exhaust system.

The Coopers, father and son, refined the 'five hundred' concept, developing the design into a production racing car, but this did not stop others working out their own ideas. However, after a short time, the cost of producing faster and faster 'five hundreds'

deterred all but the most professional. One of the most attractive approaches was devised by Paul Emery. He started with conventional specials based on Lagonda Rapier and Duesenberg engines but in 1949 he built his first 'five hundred' which looked like a miniature Grand Prix car of the time. The Emeryson had a tubular chassis and independent rubber elastic suspension. The traditional JAP engine, forward mounted,

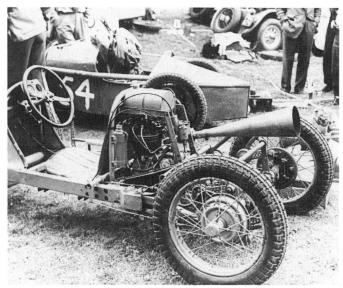

The pioneer 'five hundred': Colin Strang's special established the layout for succeeding cars in this class. The basic components were largely Fiat Topolino with power provided by a Vincent-HRD engine.

26

Paul Emery's 'Emeryson' in action at Brands Hatch in 1951. Unlike the rear-engined cars, the 'Emeryson' looked like a miniature Grand Prix car of the time.

drove the front wheels via a twin chain and gearbox train, that is Strang in reverse. The two rear wheels were fitted on brackets, no rear axle being necessary. Hydraulic brakes were fitted, but with a single inboard drum only at the front. The *Emeryson* was competitive for some years, especially with the 'Manx' Norton racing engine installed, and a number of replicas were produced before Emery returned to building larger-engined racing cars.

Other notable 'five hundreds' included JP, JBS and Kieft, all of which started life as one-offs. There were several European machines such as the Swedish *Effyh* and the French DB but the combination of the Cooper chassis, complete with disc brakes, and the very professionally prepared Norton engine resulted in the loss of the original low-cost amateur spirit.

Jim Meikle used a production Cooper to create an awe-inspiring special in 1957. The conventional motorcycle engine was replaced by a French SNECMA pulse jet, becoming in effect a four-wheel 'doodlebug'.

Sydney Allard making light work of a section of the Lawrence Cup trial in his highly successful Allard special. Although the engine was basically a Ford Model 40 V8, much of the aluminium body, the steering and the fuel tank were acquired from a damaged Bugatti. The action of the independent front suspension can clearly be seen. Despite its apparently high centre of gravity, the Allard was also successful on the track and for sand racing.

SPECIAL BUILDERS WHO BECAME MANUFACTURERS

In the back of many special builders' minds is the possibility that their car may prove a successful commercial product. This has happened only to a very few. To have any chance of success, it is necessary to combine technical excellence, commercial practicality, business acumen and necessary finance. The following are representative of the special builders who became motor manufacturers.

ALLARD

Sydney Allard, a garage owner with a Ford agency in south-west London, was a trials enthusiast. After competing with production and modified Fords, in 1934 he took a damaged Ford V8 as the basis for his special. He moved as much weight to the rear as possible for maximum traction, grafted on an old and light Bugatti Grand Prix body and raised the ground clearance. The Allard Special was an immediate success; furthermore, it looked like a real car,

not a 'bitza'. Its roadholding was improved by the installation of a split front axle, designed by L. M. Ballamy, and the car not only won many trials awards but was a potent racing car and on one occasion nearly climbed Ben Nevis. Its performance was noted and other drivers approached Allard to provide copies.

A series of Allard Specials followed, similar in concept in that they were based on Ford components, and using either Ford V8 or Lincoln V12 engines. These large American engines provided enormous torque at low speed and there were few hills the Allards could not climb. Bodywork was to customers' preference and further efforts at lightening resulted in the Allards having a maximum speed of well over 100 mph (161 km/h). The cars were not cheap — up to £650 — and by 1939 the Allard Special design had been refined so that the last of the twelve Allard Specials was a prototype production car.

Above: *The 1953 Sphinx was a combination of an Allard JR chassis and an Armstrong-Siddeley Sapphire 3.5 litre engine. It was built by Tommy Sopwith, son of Sir Thomas, whilst a postgraduate apprentice with Armstrong-Siddeley and, although the Sapphire was not normally regarded as a competition engine, the car proved a serious competitor to Jaguars in club and even national races.*

Below: *The Steyr-Allard was built in 1946 by Sydney Allard by installing an air-cooled Steyr military engine in a modified production Allard chassis. The car was modified extensively during its career: this picture, taken at Prescott hillclimb in 1954, shows it in four-wheel drive form.*

Then the Second World War intervened but by 1945 Allard had developed commercial plans for production and the Allard J1, K1 and L models were introduced in 1946. Thereafter the Allard Motor Company built over 1900 cars, ceasing production at the end of the 1950s.

In 1947 Allard reverted to special building, this time for speed hillclimb work. He based his design on a former military air-cooled 4 litre Steyr-Puch V8 engine. This was highly tuned and installed in a slimmed production Allard chassis, adapted as a single-seater. Power was transmitted via a Ford gearbox to twin rear wheels and subsequently this was modified to four-wheel drive. In the Steyr-Allard he set out to compete with the foremost hillclimbers of the day — Poore's Alfa Romeo and Raymond Mays's supercharged ERA. By a process of steady development, increasing the capacity to 4470 cc with 12-1 compression ratio, installing an electrically

29

The first Cooper, in the paddock at Prescott in 1947, where it showed considerable promise but the engine proved too powerful for its mountings. From the outset the Cooper looked a professional machine, in contrast to some of the distinctly primitive early 'five hundred' specials.

controlled gearbox and strengthening the wheels, Allard achieved his goal, winning the 1949 British National Hillclimb Championship.

COOPER

The name of Cooper has many motoring associations — Mike Hawthorn's Cooper-Bristol, Jack Brabham and the World Championship Coopers and the remarkable Mini-Coopers are just a few. John Cooper started in the motor business with his father, Charles, and during the austerity period immediately after the Second World War he became interested in the half-litre car movement. His special was designed around Fiat Topolino parts, principally two front suspension units attached to a centre frame, providing independent springing all round. Fiat steering, brakes and wheels were also

The powerhouse of the Cooper: a Norton 500 cc 'single' installed in Stirling Moss's car. The primary chain drive, clutch and gearbox are clearly visible.

used. Power was provided by a 500 cc speedway JAP engine, driven by chain via a Triumph motorcycle gearbox to a solid rear axle. The bodywork was particularly professional.

The first few outings in 1946 showed that theory and practice are not necessarily the same. Particular problems were experienced with the engine mountings, which were not strong enough for the car's performance. A transverse rubber-supported cradle solved the problem.

For 1947 a second car was built and the two Coopers dominated 500 cc racing. As a result many orders were placed for replicas for racing in what was rapidly becoming a popular form of inexpensive sport, Formula III. One was supplied to the eighteen-year-old Stirling Moss. Many hundreds of 500 cc cars were produced at the Coopers' Surbiton factory in the following years and they so dominated Formula III racing that the competitive and inexpensive aims of its sponsors were lost. Other engines were used, notably Norton and the 1000 cc twin Vincent and JAP units. Coventry Climax-engined cars followed and these led Cooper to the Formula I World Championship in 1959.

LOTUS

Colin Chapman's career also began by building specials immediately after the Second World War. An engineering student, he bought and sold old cars to supplement his income and, left with an unsaleable Austin Seven, he decided to turn it into a special. Using aircraft design principles, he rebodied the Austin in alloy-bonded plywood, which helped to render the chassis more rigid. He used the car, which he christened *Lotus*, for trials. In 1949 the Lotus Mark II followed. The chassis was also Austin with a Ford split front axle and power from a virtually new Ford Ten engine, fitted with a light alloy body. By 1950 Chapman had entered racing and found that both he and the car showed considerable promise. At the end of 1950 he sold both cars and embarked on the Lotus Mark III, designed specifically for racing in the 750 formula and powered by a much modified Austin Seven engine, special attention being paid to the inlet manifolding. The Austin chassis was strengthened by a framework or cage of tubes and an ultra lightweight body. The split-axle Ford front suspension mounted on a transverse semi-elliptic spring was retained. The result was total domination of the formula, so much so that the rules had to be changed, but not before Chapman had built a replica Mark III fitted with a Ford 1172 cc engine. Another Ford-engined trials special, the Mark IV, followed but by this time the demand for Chapman's cars was established. The upshot was the Lotus Mark VI, based on a multi-tube space frame and launched in 1952. Some of the features were retained — the split front axle and a concentration on lightness. The prototype engine was a de-stroked Ford Consul rated at 1.5 litres and from then on Chapman enjoyed enormous success. The Mark VI was in due course superseded by the Mark VII and is in effect still in production in the 1990s.

Colin Chapman's most advanced special was the Lotus Mark IIIB, seen in 1953 at a race at Ibsley for cars built to the 1172 formula. Alongside the Lotus, number 27, driven by Adam Currie, are several home-built specials, including a Buckler and Small's DHS number 29. De Souter's Lotus Mark VI is on the extreme right.

FURTHER READING

Bolster, J. V. *Specials*. Foulis, 1949.
Grant, G. *500 cc Racing*. Foulis, 1950.
Jenkinson, D. S. *Directory of Historic Racing Cars*. Aston Publications, 1987.
May, C. A. N. *Shelsley Walsh*. Foulis, 1946.
May, C. A. N. *Speed Hill Climb*. Foulis, 1962.
Stephens, P. J. *Building and Racing My 750*. Foulis, 1953.

There are also many books on individual car makes available for background information. The *RAC British Motor Sports Yearbook* contains relevant rules and regulations for each type of competitive event and the cars eligible.

WHERE TO SEE SPECIALS

Many of the specials described still survive in private ownership and some continue to be driven in competition. Details of such meetings and general information on specials are frequently published in *Motor Sport, Classic Cars* and similar journals. The following is a list of typical events where specials might be seen in action:

HILLCLIMBS
Prescott, Gloucestershire, organised by Bugatti Owners Club.
Shelsley Walsh, Worcestershire, organised by Midland Automobile Club.
Wiscombe Park, Devon, organised by Vintage Sports Car Club.

RACES
Silverstone, Northamptonshire, organised by Vintage Sports Car Club.
750 Motor Club race meetings at various venues.

SPRINTS
Brighton, East Sussex, organised by Brighton and Hove Motor Club.
Curborough, Staffordshire, organised by Vintage Sports Car Club.

TRIALS
The Exeter, Land's End and Edinburgh trials, organised by the Motor Cycling Club.

SPORTING TRIALS
High Peak Trial, organised by Sheffield and Hallamshire Car Club.
Roy Feddon Trial, organised by Bristol Motor Club and Light Car Club.

Arthur Mallock enjoyed considerable success with his Austin Seven specials, before producing a series of Ford-based U2 cars, which have proved to be highly competitive in circuit racing. Here he is seen in one of them at Silverstone in 1961.